Frankiesaurus

The stolen egg adventure

Written and published by G.L.Newman.

For my nephew, Frankie, and my niece Millie.

I hope you enjoy the story.
Love from Uncle Gary.

Created using Canva
and KDP.

Frankiesaurus was so happy to have a little sister to play with, he'd forgotten all about the other eggs.

Everyone was so excited to see what the last two eggs would produce.

This would complete their little family.

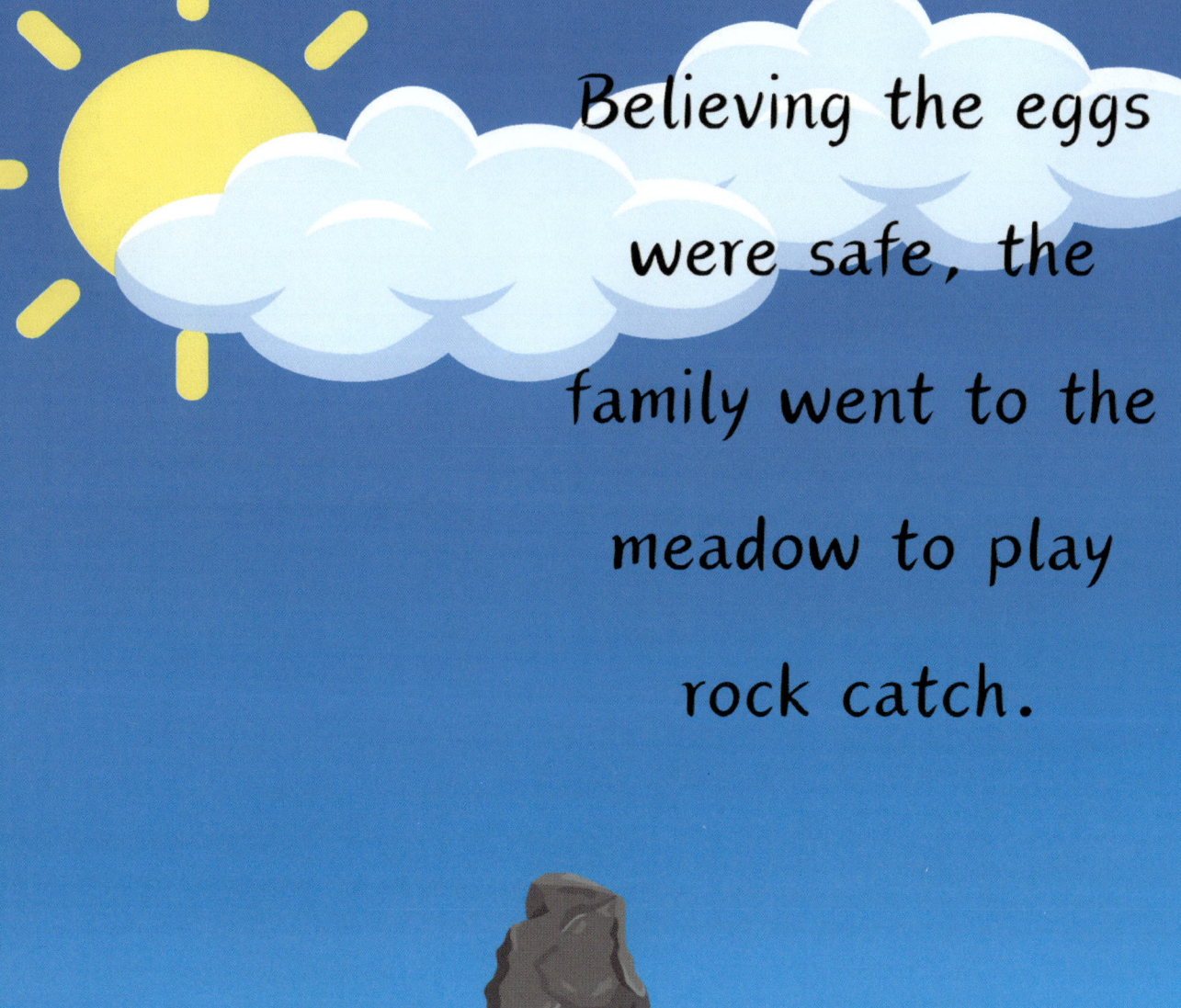

Believing the eggs were safe, the family went to the meadow to play rock catch.

A loud squawking noise made the family worried, so they raced home as fast as they could.

When they returned home, they were horrified to see one of the eggs being taken from the nest.

What were they going to do?

The missing egg made the family sad.

Mummysaurus and Daddysaurus swore never to leave the remaining egg alone ever again.

They were so scared!

Frankiesaurus took his little sister to the meadow, so his parents could be alone.

"We have to do something!"

Frankiesaurus and Milliesaurus decided to try and retrieve the stolen egg.

Yay let's do it!

They searched the ground for any clues.

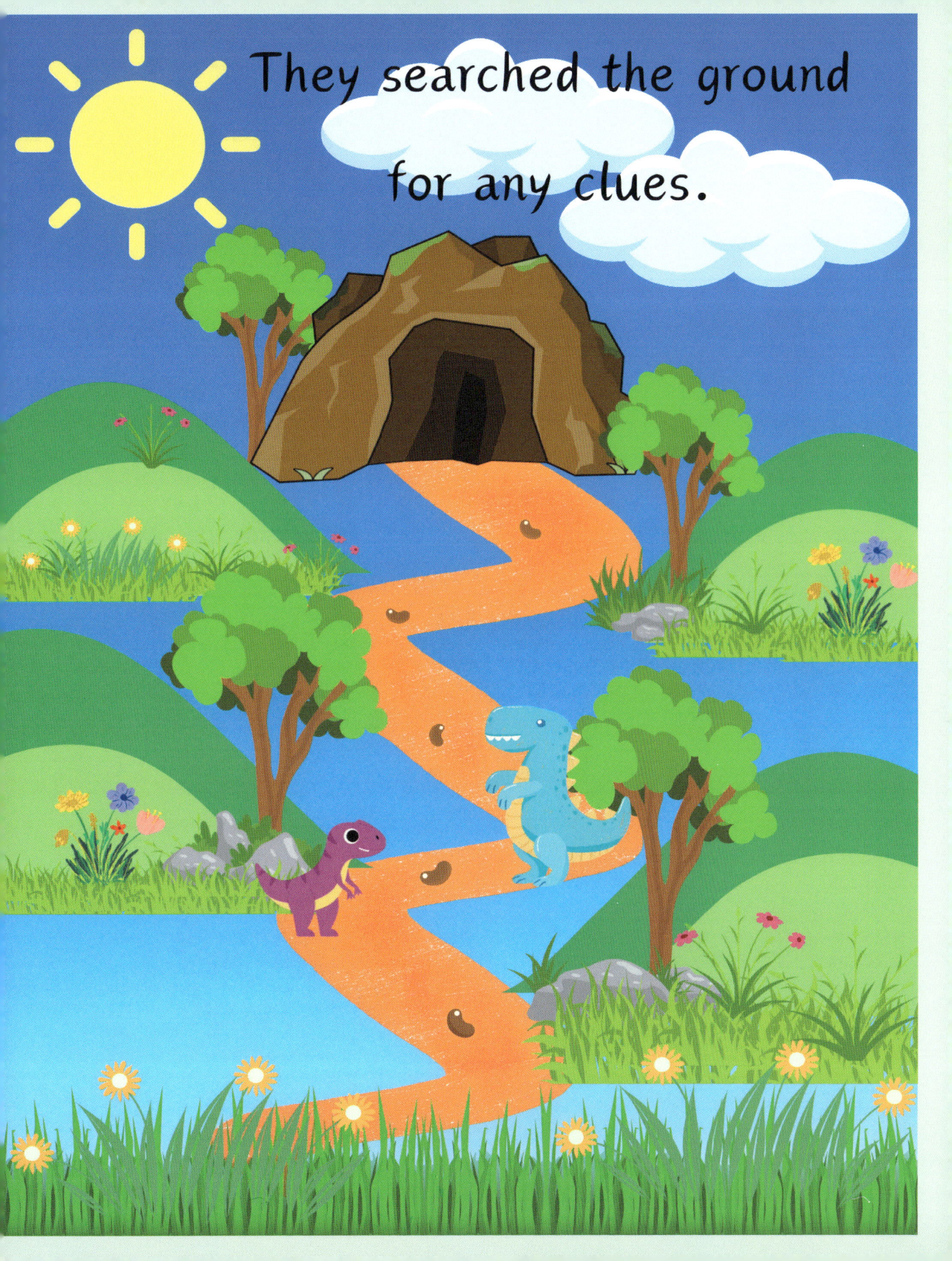

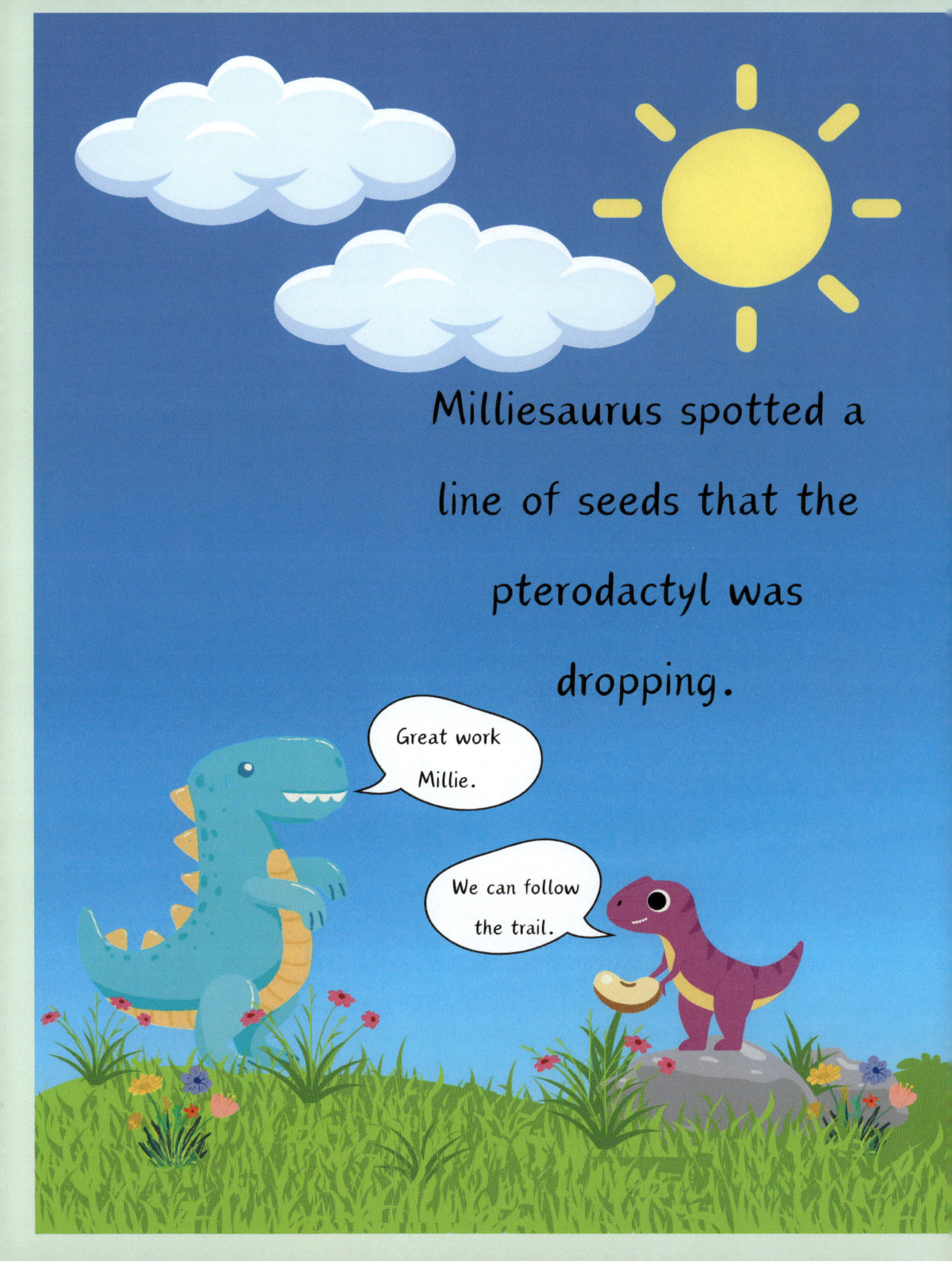

Milliesaurus spotted a line of seeds that the pterodactyl was dropping.

Great work Millie.

We can follow the trail.

They followed the path of seeds, which led them to a mountain range.

Milliesaurus spotted the stolen egg on top of the mountain.

Look up there!

When they became closer, they realised just how high the mountain was.

Some of its peaks reached high above the clouds!

There was only one way to retrieve the egg.

"Please be careful."

Milliesaurus was scared for her brothers safety.

Frankiesaurus climbed up the side of the mountain to reach the egg.

After a long climb Frankiesaurus finally reached the stolen egg.

Frankiesaurus was just about to grab the egg when he heard Milliesaurus shout something.

LOOK OUT!

Before Frankiesaurus could grab the egg, he was knocked backwards by what he thought was a gust of wind.

Woah!

After regaining his balance, he realised it was the egg thief who had flown past him so fast, he was almost knocked off the mountain.

Frankiesaurus and the pterodactyl tussled over the egg.

Milliesaurus looked on in horror. She was really worried about her big brother.

Oh no!

Frankiesaurus pulled as hard as he could. He wasn't going to let the egg slip away.

After a loud POP, the pterodactyl was sent flying through the air.

Milliesaurus was so scared, she could no longer watch.

WEEEE!

POP!

Frankiesaurus raced down the mountain with the egg.

With the egg secured, they headed back home.

Let's go home.

Yay you did it.

Mummysaurus and Daddysaurus were so happy to see their egg back home, safe and sound.

"You saved my baby."

"LOOK! Mum and Dad."

Mummuysaurs and Daddysaurus couldn't have been happier.

"Ah, my babies."

Frankiesaurus was a hero, but he couldn't have done it without the help from his little sister, Milliesaurus.

"Let's play rock catch."

"YAY!"

Printed in Great Britain
by Amazon